TOWPATH
FLOWERS

CHRIS HOWKINS

PUBLISHED BY

Chris Howkins, 70 Grange Road,
New Haw, Addlestone, Surrey
KT15 3RH.

PRINTED BY

Ian Allan Printing, Coombelands
House, Coombelands Lane,
Addlestone, Surrey KT15 1HY.

Alder catkins

ISBN 0 9519348 2 1

INTRODUCTION

Water always attracts people and when the marginal vegetation is enhanced with summer flowers, butterflies and damselflies, then it can be a very pleasant time indeed. All the flowers have their own 'biographies' and the following pages offer extracts from some of these. The entries are in no way complete but offer a variety of topics from heraldry to medicine.

The information has been collected from many sources as part of the researches into the history of the use of plants in Surrey. The plants chosen grow widely far beyond that county but anyone in Surrey wishing to discover these flowers for the first time can find all of them along the towpath of the Godalming Navigation between Godalming Wharf and the Unstead Sluices. You don't even need to walk as that is the stretch of river on which the horse-drawn narrowboat is operated by the Godalming Packet Boat Company. All these flowers can be spotted easily from on board.

Along here came such great gardeners as Gertrude Jekyll and W.R.Dykes, both local residents, who helped to popularise the horticultural use of such beauties as the Iris, Marsh Marigold and Forget-me-not. Godalming also became the home of Nathaniel Godbold who made his money using wild plants in his patent medicines, and, General James Oglethorpe, who as founder of the state of Georgia inadvertently helped introduce useful British plants into the New World.

Enjoy the flowers but remember it is illegal to pick or uproot them, especially along the Godalming towpath which is protected by the National Trust byelaws.

FLOATING SWEET GRASS

Glyceria fluitans

Fringing the watersides in high summer one of the most
conspicuous plants is the yellow green foliage of the
Floating Sweet Grass - floating because it can grow
right in the water and spread its leaves out over the
surface; sweet because of its flavour (Glyceria comes
from the Greek for sweet as per glucose). It is very
succulent to grazing cattle which will wade into the
water after it. The grass will also grow further back
from the waterside but only if the meadow is sodden so
it has limited agricultural value. It does help
protect river banks from erosion.

Few of our native grasses have seeds big enough to be
worth harvesting but this one is an exception and has
been gathered in times of dire necessity, hence its
other name of Manna-Grass (after Exodus XVI 31). It
was grown for this purpose on the Continent, being used
in soups and gruels, but was little used in Britain
although small amounts were imported for sale in
London. The husks left after preparation were kept and
fed to horses that had worms but the grass contains no
effective vermifuge; the husks were simply a mechanical
irritant to shift the worms.

It was said to be the finest food for fattening geese
and trout like it too.

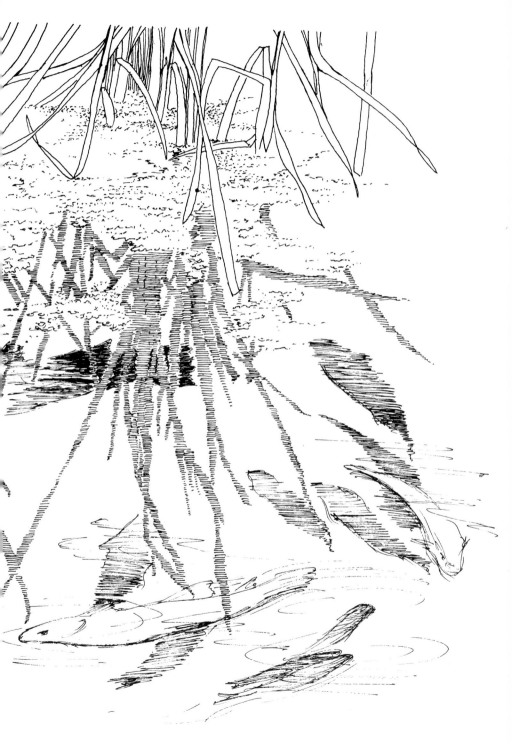

HEMLOCK WATER DROPWORT

Oenanthe crocata

Dead Man's Fingers ... Dead Man's Oatmeal ... the
country names for this plant are so much more evocative
than the clumsy great Hemlock Water Dropwort. They
have truth too, for, like the true Hemlock (Conium
maculatum) this is a very poisonous plant.

In early spring it sends up great bunches of luscious
bright green ferny leaves along the watersides and in
damp meadows from the tuberous rootstock. When farmers
used to go ditching and throw these bunches of white
tubers up on the banks with the rst of the spoil so it
got the name Dead Man's Fingers. People on hard times
tried drying them and grinding them down into meal to
cook for food. Then they found out that such treatment
does not destroy the toxic chemicals and it earned its
name of Dead Man's Oatmeal.

By June and July it is usually taller than neighbouring
plants and spreading out umbrellas of white flowers.
This helps to distinguish it from nearly five dozen
other such umbellifers in Britain. Its stems are
grooved like celery and when it is so yellow a green in
spring people have mistaken it for that vegetable,
urged on by articles encouraging the gathering of food
for free from the countryside.

6

Leave it alone. It contains oenanthetoxin which is a convulsant toxin that can be fatal to both man and beast and can strike without warning symptoms. The greatest concentrations are stored in the tubers but the greenery is poisonous too. Like so many of our poisonous plants it can be very beautiful - the banks of it beside the River Wey opposite Godalming Wharf make a glorious example of natural landscape gardening when their masses of white umbrellas are reflected in the water on an early summer evening.

HEMP AGRIMONY

Eupatorium cannabinum

Like most of the other
plants in this book,
the Hemp Agrimony has
to grow tall to hold its
flower heads high above other
rank riverside vegetation thriving
on the abundant moisture. Consequently
it is not until high summer that the stems
become overtopped with flattish heads of shaggy
pink flowers: a very distinctive colour in the British
flora, giving it the name Raspberries-and Cream in some
parts of the county. The little flowers mass together,
disguising the fact that they belong to the daisy
family, the largest family of flowering plants. The
genus of Eupatorium is also large, with about 400
species of which the Hemp Agrimony is the other British
one. Well known in gardens, however, is one of its
close relatives, the little blue Ageratum, used as a
summer bedding plant.

The Eupatoriums have been described as some of the
most important plants used in herbal medicine. The
bitterness of Hemp Agrimony served as a digestive tonic
and to purify the blood, especially in spring when
people were debilitated after a mean winter diet.
Taken in heavier doses it cleared the body out
altogether but take too much and its laxative and
emetic qualities may act more powerfully than desired.
It had other uses too.

It may also have fungicidal and insecticidal qualities
as there is a tradition that bread was wrapped in the
leaves to stop it going mouldy and that burning leaves
would rid the house of insects.

The names 'hemp' and 'cannabinum' come from the slight similarity in the leaves between this plant and the true hemp, Cannabis sativa. The latter was well-known, being a standard field crop in Surrey and many other counties. It was used for providing the hemp fibre used for rope-making and for the strong coarse cloth the Victorians named hessian. Today the name hessian conjures up thoughts of sacking or wall covering whereas earlier people used it for all manner of cheap cloth, from clothing to bed sheets. It was an important product in the medieval economy, occuring regularly on lists of tithes paid to the Church. Nowadays it is illegal to grow it or possess it due to drug abuse of its resin.

The connection with ropes, by name only, has brought about the 'tradition' that Hemp Agrimony provided the material from which were mdade the ropes to bind Christ to the Cross; hence one of its English names being 'Holy Rope'. There is no evidence that this plant was ever used as a source of fibre, whether for ropes or for textiles.

The name of the genus is the ancient name for the plant as used by Pliny and Dioscorides. It derives from a Mithridates Eupator, who was a King of Pontus (Persia), in the 1st century BC. He was famed for his herbal knowledge and in particular for his claim that a species of this genus yielded an antidote against poisons.

In the past the Eupatoriums were held in high esteem. In the 18th century the Surrey nurseryman John Cree, of Addlestone, introduced many new plants into cultivation. These included "two new Eupatoriums", to be found on an invoice of 1768 to one of his best customers, Her Royal Highness the Dowager Princess of Wales, who was building up the garden that was to develop into the Royal Botanic Gardens, Kew. She had to pay dearly for these new treasures - four shillings. Today our native Hemp Agrimony is available for garden use, at reasonable cost, from several national growers.

HORSERADISH

Armoracia rustican

Horseradish, from which is made the tasty condiment to roast beef, looks like a tall bright green Dock for it has ferocious tap roots to ensure its survival. Just below Trowers Bridge on the Godalming Navigation grows a fine clump, between the towpath and the water, sending up tall, smooth leaves which distinguish it from the coarse blue-green leaves of the Comfrey around it. This clump flowers regularly, which is more than many do, so in early summer look for the tall sprays of white bloom made up of little florets.

Originating from S.E. Europe, the plant was first used for medicine although it is said to have been one of the five bitter herbs eaten by Jews at the Feast of the Passover. By the 16th century the Danes, and even more so the Germans, had started making a condiment from it, for fish. By about 1640 it was being so used in this country when Parkinson was able to report usage by the Germans and by the labourers of England, 'for it is too strong for tender and gentle stomaches.'

It's certainly strong and so attracted, inevitably, folk-lore such as it being keenest when dug during a full moon - recorded from Godalming in 1973. The taste is due to the action of two constituents in the plant: a glycoside called sinigrin and the enzyme myrosin. These are kept separate in the cells but get mixed when the plant is bruised and cut for use. Then the myrosin decomposes the sinigrin into mustard oil. Too much of that burns and blisters skin and soft tissue. Cattle, ponies and pigs have all died from eating it. It has been popular as a powerful emetic and to shift worms out of children. Germs don't like it either so it has antiseptic properties, counteracting the effects of bad meat in former days, when used as a condiment.

DO NOT USE during pregnancy, kidney or thyroid problems or if it causes diarrhoea and night sweating.

Above : Female Orange Tip
   Butterfly; enlarged.
Above left: Garden Carpet Moth.
   Larvae of both will feed on
Horseradish.

Leaves - larger than Dock at 50 cm. Bright green wavy edge. Savage taste.

Roots - from which the condiment is made.

11

LADY'S SMOCK

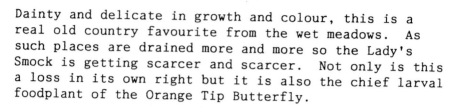

Cardamine pratensis

Dainty and delicate in growth and colour, this is a real old country favourite from the wet meadows. As such places are drained more and more so the Lady's Smock is getting scarcer and scarcer. Not only is this a loss in its own right but it is also the chief larval foodplant of the Orange Tip Butterfly.

Its popularity has earned it many names, which makes research all the more difficult. In the Middle Ages it was known either as Flos Cuculi which is now used for the Ragged Robin (Lychnis), or, Nasturtium aquaticum minus, or Lesser Watercress and those names have been transferred too. With the development of white linen a similarity was seen between the sheets of bloom and the laundry spread out on the bleaching greens so names such as Lady's Smocks, Ladies' Smocks, Smell Smocks came into being. These were originally Christianised as Our Lady's Smocks etc. but after the Reformation the Catholic allusion to the Virgin Mary was dropped. Thus in Tudor times it became Impatient Lady's Smocks because the explosive seed pods barely wait to be touched before dispersing their contents. Cuckoo Flower, shared with other plants, arose from the time of flowering, just as the people of Norfolk called it Canterbury Bells due to its flowering at the time pilgrims set off to Canterbury with the bells on their horse harness announcing their passing.

It used to be grown as Bitter Cress (a different group of plants today) because it tastes like Watercress and was added to salads, soups and the cooking pot. Any surplus was sold on the market stalls, especially in Sweden and Germany (Saxony and Bohemia). It is safe to use today but many will dislike the taste it leaves behind; best to stick to Watercress! It is a source of minerals and vitamins, especially vitamin C hence its former use as an antiscorbutic.

Gertrude Jekyll wrote, "I am very fond of the double Cuckoo-flower. It has such a clean, fresh, look and the doubling makes such a pretty round rose-shaped flower of each little bloom," (Home and Garden). She describes being given some from a local meadow and of a sample being taken to the Royal Horticultural Society where it received Commendation and was named after her. She loved the wild single one too.

17th century milkmaid: note costume, style of bucket and the hoop to stop them knocking against her knees.

MARSH MARIGOLDS

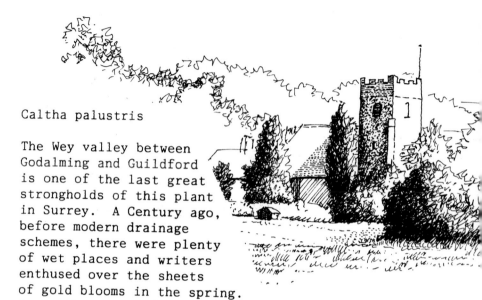

Caltha palustris

The Wey valley between
Godalming and Guildford
is one of the last great
strongholds of this plant
in Surrey. A Century ago,
before modern drainage
schemes, there were plenty
of wet places and writers
enthused over the sheets
of gold blooms in the spring.
Among them was Godalming's Gertrude Jekyll who added
that "they are largest and handsomest in the alder-
swamps of our valley bottoms, where their great
luscious clumps rise out of pools of black mud and
water."
  (from 'Wood and Garden')

The generic name comes from the Greek calathos for a
cup or goblet. Kingcups is another Surrey name
although in 19th century Farnham they were known as
Broad Buttercups, as recorded by George Sturt in his
'Small Boy in the Sixties', (ch.IX)

The flowers last a long time as the stamens ripen in
sequence, rather than all together, and as there are
about 100 of them this takes time. The flowers were
strewn at cottage doorways and made into garlands for
the May Day celebrations. Presumably this was not
simply due to their abundant beauty and colour but to
a deeper significance because a tradition persisted
that if they were hung over stable doors they would
ward off evil spirits.

The plant became Christianised and it has since been said that Marigold is a contraction of (St.) Mary's Gold whereas if fact it comes from the Saxon for 'marsh gold'; thus to call them Marsh Marigolds is to say the same thing twice. Easter Day, before the Reformation, saw the petals being strewn like carpets in churches.

In times of need, people have tried putting all sorts of wild plants into the cooking pot. The luscious spring growth of this plant was irresistable but alas it contains toxins of the protoanemonine group and it has killed some of those who tried it as a pot herb.

Botanically the flowers are among the most primitive in Britain. The plant is so hardy that it is believed, by some, to have persisted in southern Britain through the Ice Ages.

MEADOWSWEET

Filipendula ulmaria

People have always wanted a pleasant smell about the house and the use of aromatic plants has been a popular way of achieving this. Today we can imitate these synthetically in spray cans but only a limited choice are popular commercially, primarily pine or lemon. Formerly, however, the countryside yielded some forty popular fragrances, from plants called 'strewing herbs'. These could be strewn on the fire to release aromatic smoke, burned in special containers like incense; strewn in linen drawers, or strewn on the floor to release aromas when trodden upon. The different plants were used in different ways and released different scents. Some had added value for being insect repellant etc.

Meadowsweet could be described as the most exalted because it was the favourite of Queen Elizabeth I, who decreed that it should be strewn (on floors) in her private chambers wherever she went. Thus a county like Surrey, with its Tudor palaces and noble houses, hosted Her Majesty often and all wet areas, including the Wey valley, would have been searched for this herb.

Contrary to popular belief it was not the sweetly scented flower heads that were used. These have evolved to attract insects for pollination and when the flowers are picked a chemical reaction changes the sweetness to pungency, deterring insects from wasting their time pollinating flowers that will never produce seeds. What the Tudor workmen collected was the greenery which has a totally different aroma from the flowers. Crush a juicy leaf and you will recognise the smell from a familiar antiseptic cream! You'll wonder how it could have been her favourite when she was having other aromatic antiseptic plants, like lavender, grown for her use. Should it be winter then the roots were unearthed and from these comes yet another aroma.

Meadowsweet and willow leaves have both been used in country remedies for hundreds of years to relieve pain, especially headaches and aching joints. This was investigated early last century and from the willow, Salix alba, was isolated, in 1827, a chemical they named 'salicin' after the Salix. This led to further investigations so that Meadowsweet was found to contain methyl salicylate and salicylaldehyde. The salicylic glycosides included one that was named spiraein after the Meadowsweet which was at that time classified as a Spiraea.

The 1838 discovery, by the Italian chemist Raffaele Piria, included the knowledge that when the salicylic aldehyde was oxidized it produced salicylic acid. By 1853 Charles Frederick Gerhardt of Strasbourg was using this with acetic acid to produce acetyl-salicylic acid and by 1899 this was being produced in Germany as 'aspirin', taking its name from Spiraea.

Aspirin has been of major benefit throughout the world to sufferers of arthritis and rheumatism and now appears to be of value in the treatment of coronary artery disease. In herbalism it has a great range of uses. many valid from ancient times. Was it pure whim that in Welsh mythology the most beautiful maiden was created out of the flowers of such potent herbs as the broom, the oak and the Meadowsweet? With due ceremony she was named Blodefedd (Blodwyn) which means 'flowers'.

17

PURPLE LOOSESTRIFE

Lythrum salicaria

If you have ever wondered what it takes to get a
scientist excited than take note of this plant.
Charles Darwin wrote to Dr Gray, "I am almost stark,
staring mad over lythrum. For the love of Heaven, have
a look at some of your species, and if you can get me
some seed, do!"

Darwin had discovered that the plant is trimorphic - in
other words there are three different types of flowers,
each on a separate plant. The differences are in the
sex organs and control fertilization. Those flowers
with long styles have half their stamens short and half
are of medium length. Those with medium length styles
have half the stamens longer and half shorter than the
style while those with short styles have long and
medium length stamens. The size of the pollen grain
varies also; long stamens have large grains, medium
stamens have medium grains and short stamens have small
grains. This gives rise to eighteen differing
combinations for pollination. Darwin went on to
discover that only six gave rise to complete fertility;
those matching short with short, medium with medium and
long with long. As these never occur on the same plant
self-pollination is impossible.

To ensure cross-pollination the plant secretes nectar
at the fleshy base of the flower to attract bees, and
to help them find it, provides them with guide lines on
the petals.

18

The nectar must be very welcome too as the Purple
Loosestrife sends up its tall spikes of flowers from
mid-summer onwards when there is little else in full
bloom. Despite all this effort to ensure fertility the
plant is never found in any abundance. This is partly
because the seed must fall on bare ground and not be
buried or shaded because exposure to light is essential
for germination. Something to remember when sowing
seed for garden use; there are at least six garden
strains plus the wild species. Gertrude Jekyll, who
would have known the riverside plants at Godalming,
recommended them to use in large masses at the edge of
pond or pool," ("Wall and Water Gardens")

Medicinally, the Purple Loosestrife has active
ingredients which make it antibacterial so it has been
used widely, from gargles and mouth washes to wound
cleansing. In particular it has proved effective for
eye conditions while down in the gut it fights mild
food poisoning and chronic diarrhoea. The Irish
esteemed this cure for diarrhoea while the Swiss and
other Continentals have found it effective during
outbreaks of dysentery.

RAGWORT

Senecio jacobaea

Ragwort is one of the most
important poisonous plants in
Britain. It causes economic losses,
through death of livestock, as great
as all the other poisonous plants put together.
Humans are not at risk as it is so smelly and
unpalatable; the risk from contaminated milk is
"considered to be slight", but in the USA there
is concern over honey, although if contaminated
it would be dark yellow, smelly and unpalatable.

The Weeds Act 1959 designated Ragwort as injurious and
so under the provisions of the Act landowners are
required to prevent it spreading, risking prosecution
and fines for failure to do so. Nevertheless it is a
very common weed, especially in ill-managed pastures.
All too often these are horse paddocks and yet horses
are one of the animals most at risk, for they, like
cattle, will graze Ragwort when grass is lacking. The
toxic chemicals are pyrrolizidine alkaloids of which
the most toxic are cyclic diesters which attack the
digestive and nervous system, especially the liver.
It can take days, weeks or months before symptoms start
to show which is why it was not until 1906 that the
cause was established. It was then known as Pictou
Disease after an outbreak at Pictou in Nova Scotia
where Ragwort had been introduced from Scotland in
1852. Winton and Molteno also gave their names to the
disease. The first British case was identified in 1917
but Ragwort was held in suspicion long before that.
Ironically, it was Ragwort that was used against the
staggers in horses, hence the name Staggerwort. The
plant has at least fifteen English names, including
Stammerwort which suggests it was used for speech
therapy but this cannot be traced at present.

Ragwort is one of the foodplants
of the Common Pug Moth but it is
the orange and black banded larvae
of the Cinnabar Moth that are
better known. It doesn't take very
many of those to defoliate a
whole Ragwort plant and they
help to control the plant.
They themselves are at risk
from the parasitic braconid
wasp Apanteles popularis.

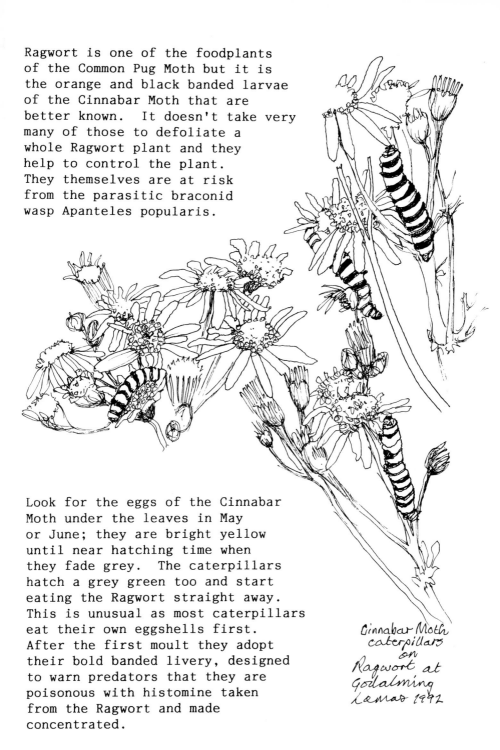

Look for the eggs of the Cinnabar
Moth under the leaves in May
or June; they are bright yellow
until near hatching time when
they fade grey. The caterpillars
hatch a grey green too and start
eating the Ragwort straight away.
This is unusual as most caterpillars
eat their own eggshells first.
After the first moult they adopt
their bold banded livery, designed
to warn predators that they are
poisonous with histomine taken
from the Ragwort and made
concentrated.

Cinnabar Moth
caterpillars
on
Ragwort at
Godalming
Lamas 1992

21

TANSY

Tanacetum vulgare

Once seen, never forgotten -
the rich green ferny leaves
of the Tansy, running up to
tall straight stems topped
with flat heads of bright
yellow buttons in high summer,
are quite unmistakeable.

It would take many pages of describe all the uses to
which man has put this plant. The strong bitter taste
made it an English 'spice', used in the sweet-and-sour
range of flavourings for medieval meals. In particular
its juice was used in the highly esteemed Tansy Cakes,
made of eggs like an omelette or pancake. The first
Shrove Tuesday pancakes were so flavoured and at the
end of the Lenten fast Tanzy's tonic qualities were
used to revive the numbed appetite. It was encouraged
by the Catholic Church as a way of commemorating the
bitter sufferings of Christ and to remember the bitter
herbs used by the Jews at the Feast of the Passover.
Then the Church started to restrict its use.

Later, the apothecary Nicholas Culpeper (1615-54) used
this as an excuse to lash out at the Physicians with
whom the Apothecaries were in dispute. At some length
he dared to write in his herbal that with "the world
being over-run with Popery" the "Physicians seeing the
Pope and his imps selfish, they began to be so too; and
now, forsooth, tansies must be eaten only on Palm and
Easter Sundays, and their neighbour days."

Thus the herb had nearly fallen from use, to the
advantage of the Physicians he claimed, because, "for
want of eating this herb in spring makes people sickly
in summer and that makes work for the physician."

Tansy contains pyrethins which are insect repellant so it was strewn around homes, put in dog kennels to deter fleas, rubbed on meat to keep flies off, etc. For the same reason corpses were treated with it to preserve them from worms - the name Tansy and Tanacetum come from the Greek 'anthanatos' meaning immortal. Intestinal worms in the living were treated with Tansy too and Culpeper thought it far safer than some of the other remedies then on offer, which he decried as being responsble for "half the defective teeth in young people". Tansy was much used to fight tooth decay.

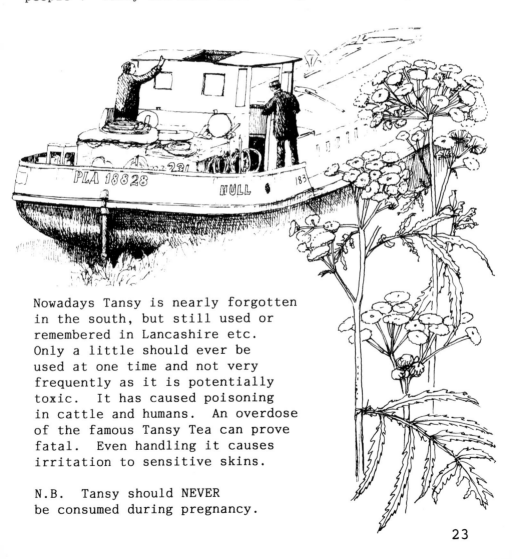

Nowadays Tansy is nearly forgotten in the south, but still used or remembered in Lancashire etc. Only a little should ever be used at one time and not very frequently as it is potentially toxic. It has caused poisoning in cattle and humans. An overdose of the famous Tansy Tea can prove fatal. Even handling it causes irritation to sensitive skins.

N.B. Tansy should NEVER be consumed during pregnancy.

23

WATER FORGET-ME-NOT

Myosotis scorpioides

"The banks of running water where the lovely Water Forget-me-not grows..." did not escape the notice of Gertrude Jekyll and she went on to work them into her planting schemes, mixing them with ferns along the waterside. (See her "Wall and Water Gardens")

The modern strains for bedding under tulips (also recommended by Gertrude Jekyll) are derived from other species and their hybrids. Myositis alpestris was introduced from Switzerland in 1818, followed by M. dissitiflora in 1868. Before these dates the Forget-me-not offered in seed catalogues, such as Loddiges of Hackney in 1804, are believed to be this wild Water Forget-me-not.

In other words there were no Forget-me-nots in general cultivation until early last century. The name was known, however, because country people used it for the Speedwell, Veronica chamaedrys. This has caused a lot of confusion for historians who are interested in the flower because it became a royal emblem. Where the flower is actually depicted in some way the two can be distinguished because the Veronica has four pointed petals whereas the Myosotis has five founded ones.

Henry of Lancaster, Earl of Derby, took the French motto "Soveigne Vous de Moy" (Forget me not) as his motto about 1390 and with it the flower emblem. He needed to be remembered as he had a claim to the throne but not the strongest. Nevertheless he acceded as Henry IV. His Lancastrian supporters wore a collar of linked S letters (for Soveigne; easily mistaken for Sovereign) with the flower emblem between them. Thus the four petals reveal the motif as the Veronica   The Lord Mayor of London sometimes wears such a collar on ceremonial occasions, one having been given to the City in 1525.

With this in mind we can dismiss romantic tales explaining the origin of the name ....Once upon a time a German knight was walking with his true love along the banks of the Danube when he decided to pick her some flowers. Alas, he sank into the river under the weight of his armour, just having time to throw her the flowers and shout "Forget-me-not." What a superman though - to manage a country ramble while clad in plate armour!

Another amusing notion, going back to the ancient Greeks, was that drinking wine in which the plant had been boiled would stop you being bitten by scorpions and other venomous beasts. This notion was duly passed on to the English in Gerard's herbal of 1597 and today the plant carries the specific name scorpioides in commemoration. In deciding which plant to use the choice fell upon the Forget-me-not because its flower stalk arches over like a scorpion's tail. Thus it was named Scorpion Grass.

Later herbalists used it against eye complaints while today's homeopaths use it for respiratory problems. The rest of us enjoy it for being simply "the blue and bright-eyed floweret of the brook." (Coleridge 1802)

WEY BALSAM

Impatiens glandulifera

Come high summer, when the rest of the riverside
flowers have gone to seed, then this plant provides a
feast of nectar for the bumble bees, honey bees and
hover flies. It is able to support such a wide range
of wildlife because it has no clever floral structures
to keep them out. Many British plants have developed
such structures to ensure pollination by specific
species of insect but this is a foreign plant.

It was brought from India for garden use in 1839 and
since then it has escaped to the wild. Few Indian
plants are hardy in Britain unless, like this one, they
come from high in the frosty mountains, hence one its
other names is Himalayan Balsam. It overwinters as
seed, which germinates early in the year. The
seedlings grow with great speed to outstrip all other
plants and shade them out from a height of two metres
or more.

Surrey was one of the places where it grew wild at an
early date, giving rise to the name Wey Balsam. As a
relative newcomer to the British flora it has attracted
a surprising number of descriptive English names such
as Giant Balsam, Indian Balsam, Policeman's Helmet,
Jumping Jack and Touch-me-not. A sideways view of the
flower, as per one in the illustration, explains the
name Policeman's Helmet, while Jumping Jack and Touch-
me-not refer to the way the yellowing ripening seed
pods will explode if squeezed. The way the pod squirms
between the fingers as it rolls back makes it feel
alive and the impact of seeds in the face is just as
disarming. Purists object to this plant being called
Touch-me-not because it is a translation of noli-
tangere and Impatiens noli-tangere is a different plant
altogether, a rarity in southern England and recorded
from only one place in Surrey. What can be found on
the Godalming Navigation, below Trowers Bridge, is the
Orange Balsam or Jewel Weed, Impatiens capensis.

WINTERCRESS

Barbarea vulgaris

Although not the best known
waterside plant it is unmistakeable.
In early spring it sends up a stem a
foot or more high bearing heads of small
cross-shaped bright sharp yellow flowers.
Below is a clump of leaves, very dark and
very shiny. They taste of watercress and were
once widely used as a winter salad. They are not
killed off by severe winters. Indeed, in countries
like Sweden, where the cold can kill cabbages, this was
the main winter green, boiled and eaten like cabbage.

It is a very healthy food, being rich in vitamin C (and
vitamin A) and having an antiscorbutic effect to
counteract the skin complaints arising from a winter
diet of salt fish and meat. Scurvy and other related
disorders were once widespread among country people by
the end of the winter. This was worse in England than
on the Continent because the English have always been
reluctant to eat their 'greens'. thus, in 1862, when
C.P.Johnson was writing about this plant he intoned
that "It would be well if the clergy, land-owners, and
other persons of influence in rural districts, would
acquire sufficient knowledge of our
native plants to enable them to point
out to their more ignorant brethren
the properties of the wild herbs
around them, and direct their attention
to those species which furnished
sustenance to their forefathers, and,
still employed for similar purposes
abroad, might often prove valuable to
themselves in periods of dearth and want."
(The Useful Plants of Great Britain)

Barbarea vulgaris is a native plant but nowadays, the
quest for the less common, is rediscovering a close
relative, Barbarea verna. Although widely distributed
as a wild plant in Surrey it is in fact an introduced
plant, coming from the Mediterranean region, so it may
well have come with the Romans. It is sold usually
under the name Land Cress but is also called Early
Wintercress and Spring Watercress. It has been more
popular in the USA, where it was also introduced and
become naturalised, so that another name is American
Cress. It has the disadvantage of needing winter
protection against the worst frosts.

It is named Barbarea after St. Barbara, one of
the 14 Auxilliary Saints or Holy Helpers,
because either the green leaves came into use
on her Feast Day, December 4th, or, because
that was the day to sow the seed. The protection
of St. Barbara was invoked during thunderstorms
and so with the invention of firearms she
became the patron saint of artillerymen.

Cows love it; horses won't touch it.

YELLOW IRIS

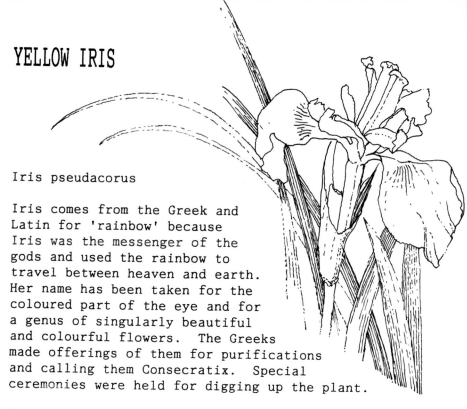

Iris pseudacorus

Iris comes from the Greek and
Latin for 'rainbow' because
Iris was the messenger of the
gods and used the rainbow to
travel between heaven and earth.
Her name has been taken for the
coloured part of the eye and for
a genus of singularly beautiful
and colourful flowers. The Greeks
made offerings of them for purifications
and calling them Consecratix. Special
ceremonies were held for digging up the plant.

Gertrude Jekyll thought this Yellow Flag Iris was
"a conspicuously beautiful plant" and know it well all
along the Godalming Navigation. She helped to
popularise them as garden plants but the person who
first demonstrated their garden worthiness was a master
at Charterhouse, also in Godalming. He was William
Dykes who developed a passion for Irises, had two
gardens of them, travelled to collect new ones for
study, bred new hybrids, became the world expert of
them and wrote the monumental monograph 'The Genus
Iris' which is still the standard work.

The violet scented and flavoured 'Orris Root' is made
from certain Irises but not the British Yellow Flag.
Nevertheless, its aromatic rhizomes were used formerly
for scenting linen drawers and laundry water. More
valuable in the late Middle Ages was the green dye from
the flowers mixed with alum, that was popular with
manuscript painters as it was cheaper than genuine
verdigris.

Orris root has been much used in dental products for centuries and slices of the rhizome held between the teeth were said to relieve toothache but avoid trying this as blistering of the gums and mouth can result. It was suspected of being poisonous back in the 18th century but our knowledge of this is still incomplete. Gardeners are warned that the juice on their hands can make some skins photosensitive. Gerard in his famous 16th century herbal warned agains this when detailing its use as a cosmetic for bruised faces.

Those same poisonous effects have been much used in medicine as a powerful cathartic; evidently 80 drops of the juice will "evacuate the intestines" when all else has failed. Similarly, the powdered rhizome was used as snuff "to excite sneezing and thus relieve pains in the head." It was believed to cure poisons too for back in the 18th century, Dr. Withering, famous for putting digitalin from Foxgloves into modern medicine, noted that the yellow iris had cured pigs bitten by a mad dog.

Varying traditions assert that the Yellow Flag Iris gave rise to the fleur-de-lys emblem of France. Three gold fleur-de-lys became the device of the Kings of France, supposedly chosen by Louis VII in his Crusade to the Holy Land. As France and England were shared they became part of the English royal arms too and persisted long after England had lost its French lands because England still claimed the right to them. Indeed the fleur-de-lys stayed on the English royal arms right up to 1800.

INDEX OF MAIN PLANT ENTRIES

IN THE SAME SERIES:
    "VALUABLE GARDEN WEEDS"
    "PLANTS TO CELEBRATE MIDWINTER"

▼▼
FOR A LIST OF OTHER PUBLICATIONS OR A LIST OF TALKS GIVEN
TO GROUPS
Write to:
Chris Howkins, 70 Grange Road, New Haw, Surrey, KT15 3RH.
▲▲